Honey Bee

Magnifying Glass

Sweet Heart

Diving Helmet

This edition published by Lemon Drop Press,
an imprint of Scholastic Inc. 555 Broadway,
New York, N.Y 10012

Fairy

Dice

LEMON DROP
AN IMPRINT OF SCHOLASTIC INC
PRESS

Copyright © Hinkler Books Pty. Ltd. 2000
Printed 2001

ISBN:0-439-35757-8

Printed and bound in China

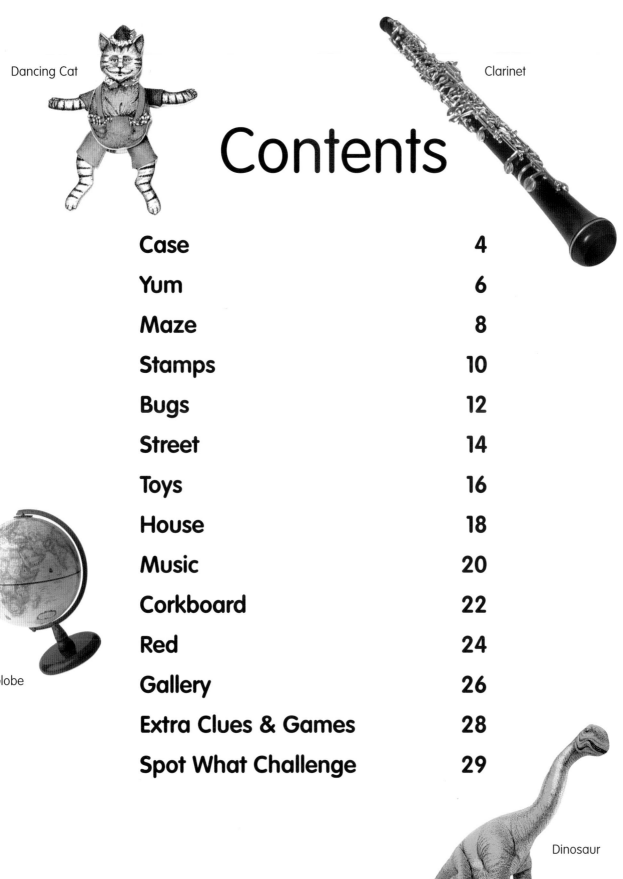

# Contents

Dancing Cat

Clarinet

Globe

Dinosaur

Collected things from many lands,
Are stored within a case.
Can you spot two clowns, a coin,
A sad and happy face,

Two ducks, two dogs, two horses,
Two ways of telling time,
Three locks, five eggs, a pumpkin head,
And a red stop sign?

Can you spot an egg of green, a white marshmallow, a gumball machine,
Two strawberries, a red candy bear, two ice-cream cones, a creamy eclair?
Find two sweet hearts, a car, a muffin, four bananas, and three tiny buttons.

spot what

Can you spot a clown
And a pear,
Four jacks, a thimble,
And a bear in a chair?

Can you find a
Tomato face,
A horse's head in
A silly place?

There's a rocket ship,
An owl in a tree,
And a way to get
From A to B.

Can you spot five paper clips
And a Chinese boat,
A rhinoceros, an elephant,
And a mountain goat?

Find the stamp from musicland
And a human brain,
A camel and a croissant,
Three different flying planes.

Can you spot a spool of thread,
A nib, a tag, and a plug,
A yacht, a die, a bolt, a key,
And a bright red ladybug?

Can you find three house flies,
A needle, and a caterpillar,
Two centipedes, two spiders,
A hook, a nail, and a gorilla?

GORILLA
BRAND

SAFETY MATCHES

13

ROOM
FOR RENT

Can you spot three arrows,
A window full of clocks,
A tiny little goldfish,
An empty flower box?

Can you find five lemons,
A camera and a cat,
A copy of this page
And a baseball bat?

Can you spot a ship
And a hungry giraffe,
A sign that says FOR SALE,
Three candles in the dark?

1716

TELEPHONE

DR. MORSE'S
Indian Root Pills

GORDON'S
PIANOS.

TRASH

Can you spot a wooden plane,
A piano, and a house,
A tractor, and a windmill,
A little wind up mouse?

Can you find three horses,
A carrot in a truck,
A tamborine, a sewing machine,
And a fluffy yellow duck?

Can you spot a pair
Of scissors,
A wagon wheel,
Shiny mirror,

A pyramid and
A clock,
A dinosaur,
A hose, a sock?

There's a happy ghost,
An old fashioned hat,
A pair of boots
And a dancing cat.

Find a saxophone, a gramophone,
A xylophone, a flute,
Four guitars, three tiny stars,
A golden harp, a lute.

Music makes the world go round,
Seven trumpets can be found,
There's a clarinet, and a ukulele too,
They all make wonderful music for you.

☺ The Bank of Smiles

To: Mother Hubbard
Address: The Shoe
Nursery Land

SPOT WHAT

01/01/2000

Account balance:

| 1/12/1999 | | |
|---|---|---|
| Deposit | | 12 laughs |
| Deposit | | 17 hugs |
| Deposit | | 34 smiles |
| Withdrawal | | 9 tears |

The more you invest in life, the more you get back from it.
A smile costs nothing, but can mean so much.

Station Street

Lower Upper Overshot Highway

stern Street

HAPPY BIRTHDAY

In cert
being
doing
destin
all,
bre
quick
and
stor
loc
p

...y most beloved,

How happy I was to ... received your last letter.
...rvellous to read all a ...
...nds very exciting. I
...en raining here alm...
...arden, but it does ma...
I've heard that others are going to follow your
    Mr. Butcher, Mr. Baker and th... local Ca...
all set off to sea in a tub no less. ...on't kn...
worthiness of such items but I'm ...re that ...
    I'm ...re you will be joining ...s as so...
... you very much and want...
...earts.

All more lo...

Quan-Yin.

NoTE

Shopping List:
4    Bones for the dog.
2    tins of dog food
1    bottle of milk
1 Packet of dog biscuits
1 Bottle of dog shampoo
Flea Powder
hair brush

sea

9th

Can you spot a spider,
A medal, and a boat,
A telephone, a turtle,
And a little love note?

Can you find a bicycle,
A violin, and feather,
A map, three green tacks,
And five kittens all together?

Can you spot
A bike and a train,
A monkey wrench
And the jet plane?

Six strawberries,
Find them all,
A pair of lips
And ping pong ball.

Can you find
A big toolbox,
A Christmas hat, and
Two Christmas socks?

Can you spot a fisherman,
A peacock, and a cat,
A racing horse, a picnic,
A dartboard, and a rat?

Can you find the television,
A tower, and a gnome,
A little yellow window
And HOME SWEET HOME?

Can you spot a vintage car,
A rabbit, and a dog,
A cow, a leaping dolphin,
And a little green frog?

Strawberry

Trumpet

See if you can spot these things in every picture:

# Can you find the words SPOT WHAT,
# A fairy, and a three,
# A matchstick, an apple,
# And a honey bee?

Ball

Jack

Rocket Ship

## Rules For The Spot What Game

**1.** Flip a coin to see who goes first.
**2.** The winner of the coin toss becomes the "caller". The "caller" chooses a picture from the book and picks something for the other person to find saying for example: "Can you Spot a knight in armor?"
**3.** The "spotter" must then find the item.
**4.** If the "spotter" can't spot it, the "caller" gets 5 points and shows her where it is. Then, the "caller" takes another turn to choose an item for the "spotter" to spot.
**5.** If the "spotter" can find the item, then she gets 5 points, and it's her turn.
**6.** The first to reach 30 points wins, but you could also set your own limit of 50 or even 100 points!

You can make the game more challenging by putting a time limit of one to three minutes on each search. Hurry up and start spotting!

Chess Piece

Keys

# The Spot What Challenge.

The following items are much harder to find so get ready for the challenge.

Creamy Eclair

### Case

(page 4/5)

Wooden Plane

Two owls
A musical note
A lizard
Two knights in armor
*The Thinker*
A viking ship

### Maze

(page 8/9)

A rainbow
4 barrels
The words, "SPOT THIS"
The words, "SPOT THAT"
A man with binoculars
3 horned helmets

Binoculars

### Yum

(page 6/7)

A bite
5 bears in a row
2 red twists
The word, "HONEY"
2 lollipops
9 balloons

### Stamps

(page 10/11)

2 leopards
2 stamps from nowhere
3 kings
A tiger
A lion
A stamp worth 4 peanuts

Wagon

Wagon Wheel

Gramophone

# Bugs
(page 12/13)

Butterfly A
Butterfly B
Butterfly C
A knight in armor
A pig
4 clown faces

# Toys
(page 16/17)

Two dinosaurs
An eggbeater
Hammer & wrench
A lion
A purse
The cow that jumped over the moon

*The Thinker*

# Street
(page 14/15)

3 shoes
6 ducks
A lantern
A scary smile
A bonsai garden
A mirror

# House
(page 18/19)

Seven keys
A fire truck
A skull
A radio
Three chess pieces
The numbers: 1, 2, 3, and 4

Ukulele

Old Radio

Pyramid

# Music

(page 20/21)

A banjo
An accordian
A pair of maracas
A bell
A tin whistle
Bongo drums

# Red

(page 24/25)

A tractor
Boltcutters
A hardhat
A feather
A clamp
2 boxing gloves

Lute

# Corkboard

(page 22/23)

9 brass tacks
"HAPPY BIRTHDAY"
Tic-Tac-Toe
A piano player
A butterfly
A helicopter

# Gallery

(page 26/27)

2 carousel horses
A gold teapot
A fork
A wrench
The letters, "OFLCTB"
The words, "THE END"

Toy Soldier

Mouse

Thimble

Chinese Boat

Magnifying Glass

# Acknowledgements

We would like to thank the following people:

**Albert Meli from Continuous Recall**

**Sam Grimmer**

**Peter Tovey Studios**

**Andrew Curtain**

**Kate Bryant**

**Tommy Z**

**Gillian Banham**

**Allison McDonald**

Rocking Horse

Nib